COMPOSER SHOWCASE
HAL LEONARD STUDENT PIANO LIBRARY

Coral Reef Suite

CONTEMPORARY PIANO SOLOS

BY CAROL KLOSE

The sea has always fascinated me—probably because I have spent most of my life in the Midwest, as far from salt water, tides, and coral reefs as one could be. This fascination has led to the *Coral Reef Suite,* which I composed to bring to life some of my favorite sea creatures, imitating them in music and motion as I remember seeing them in aquariums or in TV documentaries. These pieces are dedicated to my grandchildren Janey, Alex, Mary, and Katherine, whose love of water I hope leads them to enjoy the captivating creatures of the coral reef in person some day.

Carol Klose

CONTENTS

ISBN 978-0-634-05148-7

HAL•LEONARD® CORPORATION

7777 W. BLUEMOUND RD. P.O. BOX 13819 MILWAUKEE, WI 53213

Visit Hal Leonard Online at
www.halleonard.com

PERFORMANCE NOTES

Starfish Serenade

In this delicate waltz, imagine a starfish moving slowly and effortlessly along the sea bottom, hardly disturbing the water and sand around it. Imitate the graceful "arms" of this amazing creature by thinking in "slow motion," using smooth arm gestures as you move across the keys.

All the notes in measures 1-30 belong to a whole tone scale consisting of D-flat, E-flat, F, G, A, and B. Blend these harmonies by holding down the damper pedal without releasing. Try to picture the magical watery surroundings of the starfish as it moves gently through the notes of the whole-tone scale. Can you imagine the starfish reaching its destination as the harmony slips into the sound of D Major in measures 31 and 32?

The Jellyfish

The right-hand part in this piece imitates the movements of a jellyfish by playing clusters of white keys with graceful rising and falling motions.

Play the accompanying left-hand seconds very softly and smoothly, using the damper pedal to blend the sounds. Try to imagine the jellyfish (right hand) gliding up and down in the shimmering sea water (left hand).

Your signal to play a chord cluster is this symbol above a note. Play the written note with your right thumb, along with the four white keys above it using right-hand fingers 2, 3, 4, and 5. Play all five keys at the same time.

• Begin each cluster with a completely relaxed hand, suspended about twelve inches above the keys. Keep your fingers gently curved, so that your hand resembles the upside-down cup shape of the jellyfish.
• Drop your hand gently into the keys so that all five fingertips reach the bottom of the keybed at the same time.
• Allow your hand to rebound gently back to the starting position (about twelve inches above the keys), ready to perform the next "jellyfish" cluster. Keep your wrist flexible at all times, moving up and down as gracefully as possible.

Angelfish Arabesque

"Arabesque" is a title often given to music that has many decorative notes played quickly and smoothly. As you practice the quickly-moving eighth-note patterns in this arabesque, notice how they change directions with each left-hand cross-over. Try to imitate the graceful motion of the exotic angelfish as it swims, darting this way and that through the coral reef.

• Blend the left-hand and right-hand notes within each slur, so they sound as though played by one hand.
• Play the first note in each slur with a small impulse from behind your hand.
• Observe the crescendo and decrescendo signs carefully.
• Play with curved fingers and a flexible wrist throughout.

Ghosts Of A Sunken Pirate Ship

Once you begin this piece, you will hear a strange phenomenon: eerie sounds lingering in the air, even though you are not depressing the damper pedal and are playing staccato notes. You might even hear high pitches you did not play! Those ghostly sounds are actually sympathetic vibrations—sounds produced inside the piano by open strings vibrating in response to the vibrations of strings around them.

To bring the ghosts of your pirate ship to life, follow these easy directions:

- Before you begin the piece, silently depress the keys of the fifth shown (C and G below Middle C) with right-hand fingers 1 and 5. Hold those two keys down throughout, so the C and G strings are "open" at all times.
- Play all the remaining notes of the piece—both staves—with your left hand. Perform the left-hand cross-overs quickly and accurately, with heavily accented staccatos. The more you accent the notes, the more ghostly your sounds will be.

The Lonesome Hermit Crab

This piece is the story of a lonely little hermit crab looking for an abandoned seashell to call home. As you play his song, listen for the melody of the famous American folk tune "Home On The Range." This version, however, has a sad and woeful sound, because it is in a minor key instead of the usual major. Play this piece slowly, taking plenty of time to sound very sad and lonesome, especially in the last three measures.

The Sea Anemone

To produce the soft blended sounds necessary in this piece, hold down the damper pedal, and the una corda pedal (the left pedal) as well, from beginning to end. As you play the soft opening glissando, imagine that you are deep underwater in a clear blue-green sea. Straight ahead is a brightly-colored sea anemone, with its many tentacles swaying in the gentle current. Who would guess that those delicate tentacles occasionally reach out to capture a tiny morsel of food for the anemone? Let your fingers imitate the anemone's graceful tentacles as you play the four-note slurred patterns (such as those in measures 3-8) with fingers 1, 2, 4, and 5 in each hand. For the delicate staccatos in measures 9, 10, 17, and 18, use right-hand finger 3 and left-hand finger 3 like tentacles that pluck the food morsels from the surrounding water.

Invaders Of The Reef

Occasionally, the peaceful coral reef is threatened by invaders—perhaps sharks, barracuda, or even human beings. Use your imagination to invent the invaders, which are represented by the accented right-hand grace-note fifths in measures 4, 8, 10, and so on.

Only two different right-hand fifths are used (G-C and D-G), sometimes in different octaves. In each case, play the grace note quickly, almost at the same time as the note that follows it. Lean your arm weight into the second note of the fifth, for a strong accent.

Play with great dynamic contrast and strong accents, increasing your speed and dynamics from measure 9 on, to create even more excitement as the invaders draw near. Keep your right hand close to the keys to save time as it crosses over the left hand for the fifths in measures 15 and 16.

From measure 16 to the end, the piece becomes gradually slower and softer. Do the invaders win out, or have they come just to give the coral reef creatures a scare? Can you picture the bubbles as you play the trill on high C-sharp and D in the last measure?

STARFISH SERENADE

By CAROL KLOSE

Gentle Waltz tempo (♩ = 138)

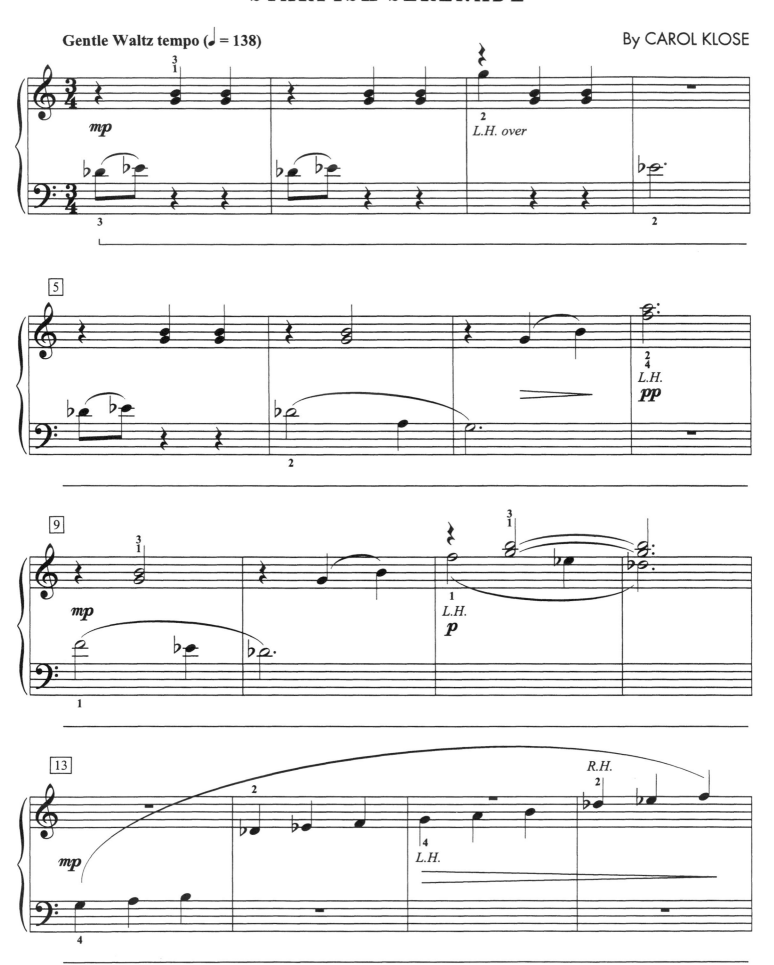

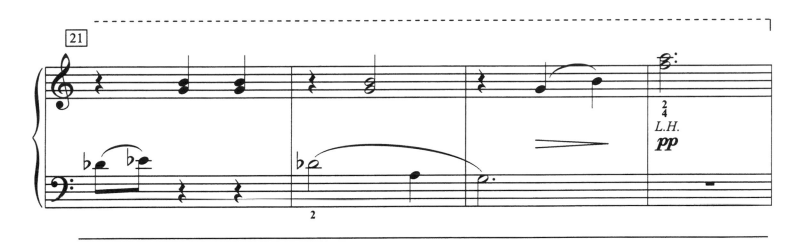

THE JELLYFISH

By CAROL KLOSE

Gracefully, in "two" (♩ = 72)

Opt. una corda pedal

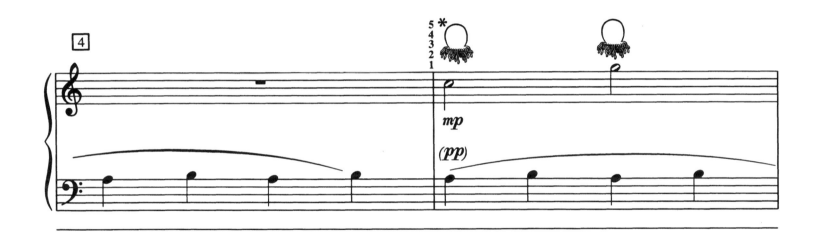

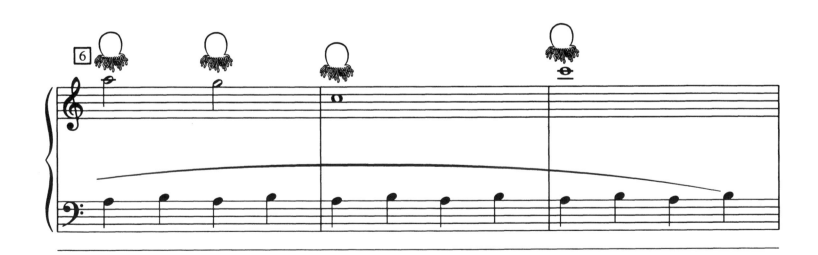

* *: Play the written note with R.H. 1 and the four white keys above it with R.H. fingers 2,3,4,5. Depress all five keys at once. Float in a large arc from one symbol to the next.*

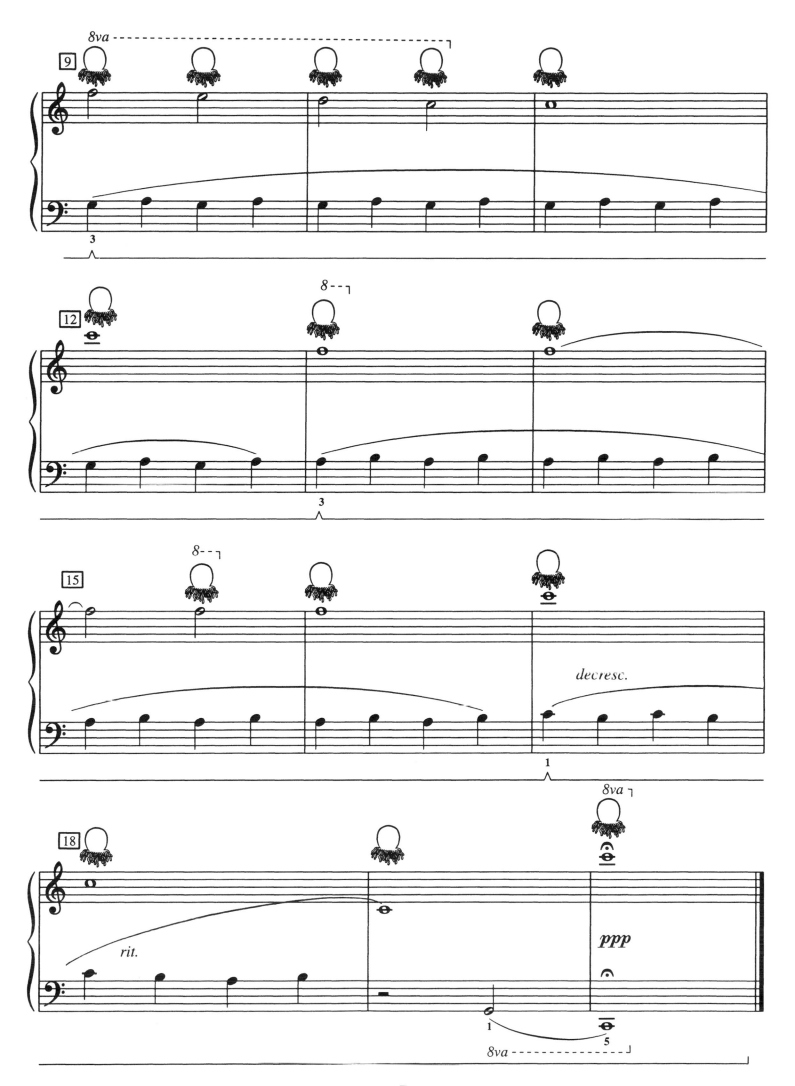

ANGELFISH ARABESQUE

By CAROL KLOSE

With motion (♩ = 160)

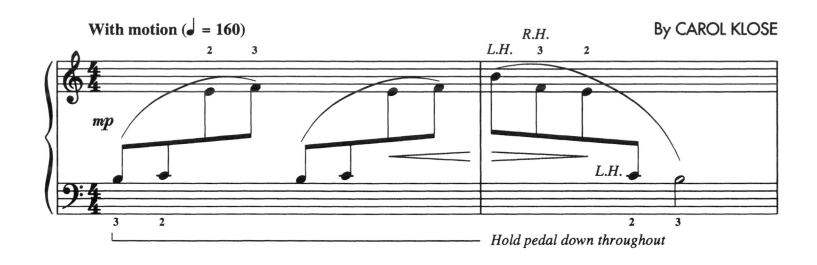

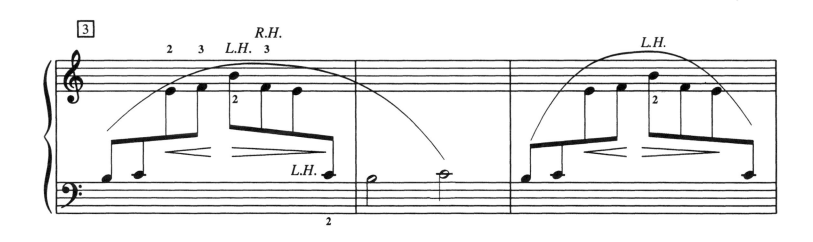

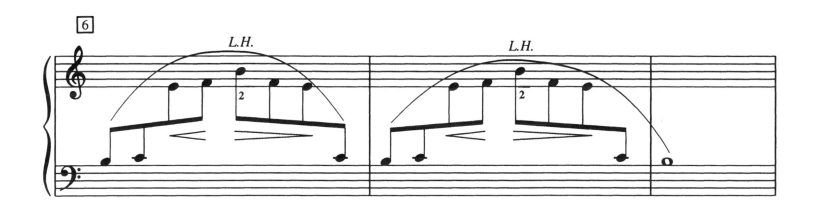

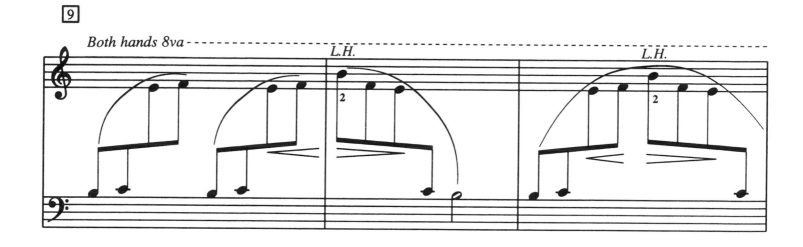

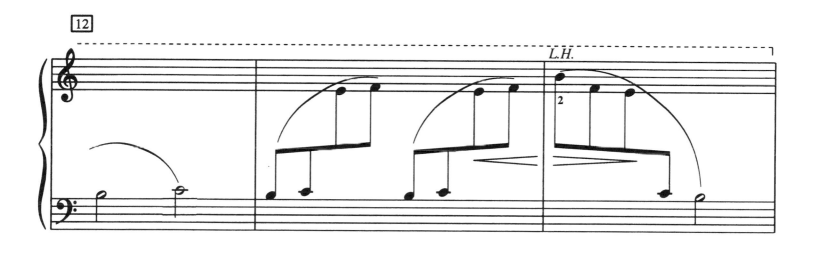

GHOSTS OF A SUNKEN PIRATE SHIP

By CAROL KLOSE

Deliberately, not too fast (♩ = 120)

Silently depress the C and G keys with your R.H. and hold them down throughout. Play the entire piece with your left hand.

(Continue to hold R.H. C and G silently until all sound fades away.)

THE LONESOME HERMIT CRAB

By CAROL KLOSE

Woefully (♩ = 72-92)

THE SEA ANEMONE

By CAROL KLOSE

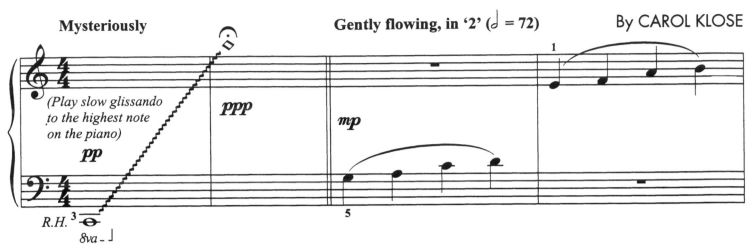

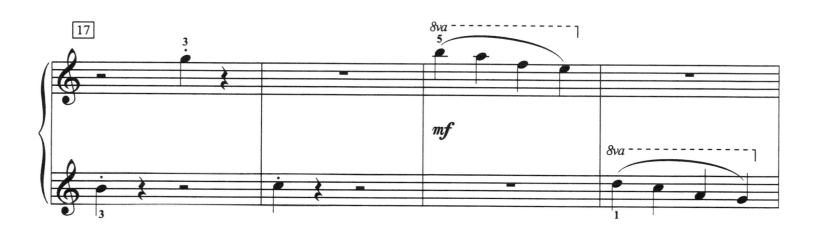

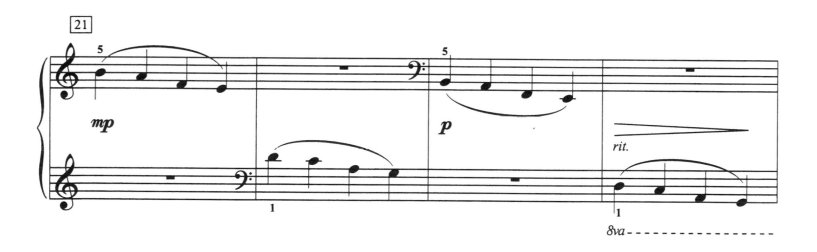

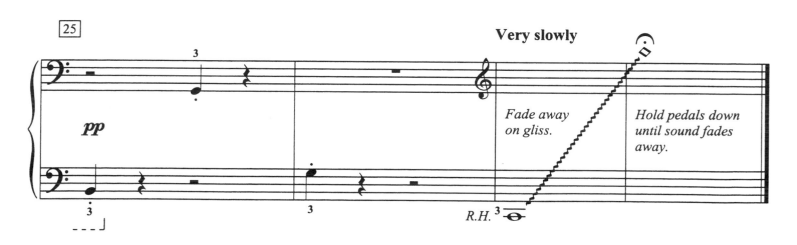

INVADERS OF THE REEF

By CAROL KLOSE

Hold damper pedal down throughout.

Hal Leonard Student Piano Library

The *Hal Leonard Student Piano Library* has great music and solid pedagogy delivered in a truly creative and comprehensive method. It's that simple. A creative approach to learning using solid pedagogy and the best music produces skilled musicians! Great music means motivated students, inspired teachers and delighted parents. It's a method that encourages practice, progress, confidence, and best of all – success.

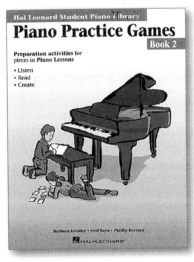 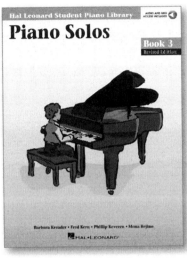  

PIANO LESSONS BOOK 1
00296177 Book/Online Audio $9.99
00296001 Book Only $7.99

PIANO PRACTICE GAMES BOOK 1
00296002 .... $7.99

PIANO SOLOS BOOK 1
00296568 Book/Online Audio $9.99
00296003 Book Only $7.99

PIANO THEORY WORKBOOK BOOK 1
00296023 .... $7.50

PIANO TECHNIQUE BOOK 1
00296563 Book/Online Audio $8.99
00296105 Book Only $7.99

NOTESPELLER FOR PIANO BOOK 1
00296088 .... $7.99

TEACHER'S GUIDE BOOK 1
00296048 .... $7.99

PIANO LESSONS BOOK 2
00296178 Book/Online Audio $9.99
00296006 Book Only $7.99

PIANO PRACTICE GAMES BOOK 2
00296007 .... $8.99

PIANO SOLOS BOOK 2
00296569 Book/Online Audio $8.99
00296008 Book Only $7.99

PIANO THEORY WORKBOOK BOOK 2
00296024 .... $7.99

PIANO TECHNIQUE BOOK 2
00296564 Book/Online Audio $8.99
00296106 Book Only $7.99

NOTESPELLER FOR PIANO BOOK 2
00296089 .... $6.99

PIANO LESSONS BOOK 3
00296179 Book/Online Audio $9.99
00296011 Book Only $7.99

PIANO PRACTICE GAMES BOOK 3
00296012 .... $7.99

PIANO SOLOS BOOK 3
00296570 Book/Online Audio $8.99
00296013 Book Only $7.99

PIANO THEORY WORKBOOK BOOK 3
00296025 .... $7.99

PIANO TECHNIQUE BOOK 3
00296565 Book/Enhanced CD Pack $8.99
00296114 Book Only $7.99

NOTESPELLER FOR PIANO BOOK 3
00296167 .... $7.99

PIANO LESSONS BOOK 4
00296180 Book/Online Audio $9.99
00296026 Book Only $7.99

PIANO PRACTICE GAMES BOOK 4
00296027 .... $6.99

PIANO SOLOS BOOK 4
00296571 Book/Online Audio $8.99
00296028 Book Only $7.99

PIANO THEORY WORKBOOK BOOK 4
00296038 .... $7.99

PIANO TECHNIQUE BOOK 4
00296566 Book/Online Audio $8.99
00296115 Book Only $7.99

PIANO LESSONS BOOK 5
00296181 Book/Online Audio $9.99
00296041 Book Only $8.99

PIANO SOLOS BOOK 5
00296572 Book/Online Audio $9.99
00296043 Book Only $7.99

PIANO THEORY WORKBOOK BOOK 5
00296042 .... $8.99

PIANO TECHNIQUE BOOK 5
00296567 Book/Online Audio $8.99
00296116 Book Only $8.99

ALL-IN-ONE PIANO LESSONS
00296761 Book A – Book/Online Audio $10.99
00296776 Book B – Book/Online Audio $10.99
00296851 Book C – Book/Online Audio $10.99
00296852 Book D – Book/Online Audio $10.99

Prices, contents, and availability subject to change without notice.

www.halleonard.com